THE
CHRISTMAS CAROL
SAMPLER

THE
CHRISTMAS
CAROL
SAMPLER

illustrated by
MARGARET CUSACK

musical arrangements by Kathleen Krull

(HBJ)

Harcourt Brace Jovanovich, Publishers
San Diego   New York   London

for Frank and Katie

Printed in the United States of America

Score design by David Dunn
Photography by Ron Breland

Library of Congress Cataloging in Publication Data
Main entry under title:

The Christmas carol sampler.

Carols with piano acc.
Contents: Joy to the world – Silent night – Jingle
bells – [etc.]
1. Carols, English.   2. Christmas music.   I. Cusack,
Margaret.   II. Krull, Kathleen.
M2114.5.C   83-6095
ISBN 0-15-217752-3

First edition

B   C   D   E

TABLE of CONTENTS

JOY TO THE WORLD

Words: Isaac Watts, 1719

Music: George F. Handel

SILENT NIGHT

Words: Joseph Mohr, 1818

Music: Franz Gruber, 1818

1. Si — lent night, ho — ly night!
2. Si — lent night, ho — ly night!
3. Si — lent night, ho — ly night!

All is calm, all is bright. 'Round yon
Shep — herds quake at the sight. Glo — ries
Son of God, love's pure light. Ra — diant

vir — gin Mo — ther and Child. Ho — ly
stream from heav — en a — far, Heav'n — ly
beams from Thy ho — ly face With the

In — fant so ten — der and mild. Sleep in heav — en — ly
hosts sing, "Al — le — lu — ia!" Christ, the Sa — vior, is
dawn of re — deem — ing grace, Je — sus, Lord at Thy

peace. Sleep in heav — en — ly peace.
born! Christ, the Sa — vior, is born!
birth, Je — sus, Lord at Thy birth.

JINGLE BELLS

James Pierpont, 1857

fun it is to ride and sing a sleigh-ing song to-night! Oh,
got in-to a drift-ed bank And we, we got up-sot.

CHORUS

Jin-gle bells, jin-gle bells, jin-gle all the way! Oh, what fun it

1.
is to ride in a one-horse o-pen sleigh,

2.
one-horse o-pen sleigh!

DECK THE HALLS

Traditional Welsh

1. Deck the halls with boughs of hol—ly,
2. See the blaz—ing Yule be—fore us,
3. Fast a—way the old year pass—es,
Fa la la la la, la la la la.

'Tis the sea—son to be jol—ly,
Strike the harp and join the cho—rus,
Hail the new, ye lads and lass—es,
Fa la la la la, la la la la.

Don we now our gay ap—par—el,
Fol—low me in mer—ry meas—ure,
Sing we joy—ous all to—geth—er,
Fa la la la la la la la la.

Troll the an—cient Yule—tide car—ol,
While I tell of Yule—tide treas—ure,
Heed—less of the wind and weath—er,
Fa la la la la, la la la la.

O COME, ALL YE FAITHFUL

Words: Translated from Latin
by Frederick Oakeley, 1852

Music: John Reading

HARK! THE HERALD ANGELS SING

Words: Charles Wesley

Music: Felix Mendelssohn

O CHRISTMAS TREE

Traditional German

AWAY IN A MANGER

Words: Martin Luther

Music: Traditional German

1. A – way in a man – ger, no crib for a bed. The little Lord Je – sus laid down His sweet head. The stars in the sky _____ looked down where He lay, The little Lord Je – sus, a – sleep in the hay.

2. The cat – tle are low – ing, the poor Ba – by wakes, But little Lord Je – sus, no cry – ing He makes. I love Thee, Lord Je – sus, look down from the sky, And stay by my cra – dle till morn – ing is nigh.

3. Be near me, Lord Je – sus, I ask Thee to stay Close by me for – ev – er and love me, I pray. Bless all the dear chil – dren in Thy ten – der care, And take us to heav – en, to live with Thee there.

WE THREE KINGS OF ORIENT ARE

John H. Hopkins, 1857

WE WISH YOU A MERRY CHRISTMAS

Traditional British

GOD REST YE MERRY GENTLEMEN

Traditional English

THE FIRST NOEL

Traditional French

THE TWELVE DAYS OF CHRISTMAS

Traditional English

On the 1. first day of Christ-mas my true love sent to me (to 1) 1. A par-tridge in a pear tree.
2. second day - etc. (to 2)
3. third day - etc. (to 3)
4. fourth day - etc. (to 4)
5. fifth day - etc. (to 5)

2. two tur-tle doves and a par-tridge in a pear tree. 3. three French hens,

two tur – tle doves, and a par – tridge in a pear tree. 4. four call – ing birds, three French hens,

two tur – tle doves, and a par – tridge in a pear tree. 5. five gold – en rings,

32

four call – ing birds, three French hens, two tur – tle doves, and a par – tridge in a pear

tree.

6. On the sixth day of Christ-mas my true love sent to me,
7. On the seventh - etc.
8. On the eighth - etc.

six geese a – lay – ing, (to 5)
seven swans a-swim-ming, (to 6)
eight maids a – milk– ing, (to 7)
nine la – dies danc-ing, (to 8)
ten lords a – leap-ing, (to 9)
eleven pi – pers pi – ping, (to 10)
twelve drum-mers drum-ming, (to 11)

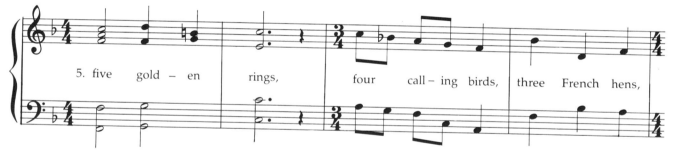

5. five gold – en rings, four call – ing birds, three French hens,

two tur – tle doves, and a par – tridge in a pear tree.

D.S.

This book was printed by offset on 80 lb. Karma Text
Separations were made by Valley Film Services
Printed by Holyoke Lithograph
Bound by A. Horowitz & Sons, Bookbinders